Get Happier, Dammit

More Inspiration and Motivation for Living in an Often-Unhappy World

Katherine Gotthardt, M.Ed.

Copyright ©2022 by ATW Publishing. All rights reserved. No part of this book may be reproduced or transmitted in any form or by any means without written permission of the author.

ISBN: 979-8-9852434-2-0

Website: GetHappyDammit.com

Cover art by Silvio Zimmermann (ballons) and Petra (background). Composition by Victor Rook.

Acknowledgements

I've been blessed with tremendous support that has allowed me to write this new and improved version of the original book *Get Happy, Dammit*. By sharing their wisdom and insights and by reassuring me when I needed it, many extraordinary people have empowered me to discover a path toward greater satisfaction in life and a means to help others. Thank you to those who contributed their ideas to make this book possible: Sima Button, Traci Carrano Jones, Timothy Horn, Cindy Brookshire, Derek Kannemeyer, Dottie Ward-Wimmer, Zach Tamer, Alexandra Mooney, Grace Joy Reid, William (Bill) Golden and others. I'm also grateful for support from Stacy Shaw, publisher of BristowBeat; Rebecca Barnes, publisher of Prince William Living; Uriah Kiser, publisher of Potomac Local News; and John Reid, publisher of PW Perspective. And thank you to the anonymous contributors who thought this project was important enough to support.

Finally, I would be remiss if I didn't mention my excellent teachers and therapists and members of Write by the Rails, the Prince William Chapter of the Virginia Writers Club. For all these people and countless more, I am grateful. You've helped me live a happier, more fulfilling life and enabled me to pass on what I have learned.

How to Use This Book

This book contains a series of essays, exercises and poems designed to help you harness the inspiration and motivation inside you and/or to help you help others. It is in no way a substitute for formal training, counseling, psychiatric treatment or medical help, and I am not a mental health professional. As you read these chapters, if you feel something is wrong in your life or the lives of those you are helping, you feel sadness or anxiety, or you feel you need support, please seek professional help right away. If you feel you want to harm yourself, please immediately call the Suicide Hotline at 988.

Dedication

To everyone in search of greater happiness. May you find the inspiration and motivation needed to achieve it, and when you do, may you share it with others.

Contents

Introduction: What's Behind Happiness? 1

Questioning Happiness 3

Get Inspired, Get Motivated 6

Do the Work 9

A Rose Isn't Always a Rose 12

What do You Need? 15

Uncovering and Nurturing the Seeds of Happiness 17

Learning to Speak in the Positive 20

What Are You Really Looking For? 23

Waking Up Is Hard To Do 26

Quit Messing Around 28

What Is It You Need to Hear? 31

More Than a Gentle Nudge 34

The Wind Knocked Out 37

Poisoning the King 40

Developing What Matters 44

The Motivation of "No Way in Hell" 47

Your Own Way Out of the Rut 51

Putting Fleeting Moments on Pause 55

Uninspiring, Unmotivating: Groupthink 58

Hanging With a New Crowd 61

It's Contagious 65

Who Are You Listening To? 68

Whatever It Takes 71

Rediscovering Your Core 75

Falling for the Fake 79
Maintenance Work 83
Conclusion 85
About the Author 87

Introduction: What's Behind Happiness?

What if you could enjoy each day a little more than you do now? You'd probably be happier, right? Most of us would be. But doesn't something have to change to make it happen? Yes. But the route to greater happiness isn't always as complicated as we believe it will be. Many times, it just takes effort and some realigning of the way we think.

If you read the original version of this book, *Get Happy, Dammit: Staying Inspired and Motivated in an Often-Unhappy World*, you might recall I focus on the ways inspiration and motivation contribute to happiness and how we have the power to build our own happiness, however we define that. The book contains short chapters with stories and poetry, along with exercises I used in the adult education classroom and in my own life. The exercises do work (and the book won a Silver Award from the Nonfiction Authors Association, which was also rather nice).

Just because the book was done didn't mean I was prepared to stop studying happiness. There's still too much to learn. But as with any learning, the way to understanding isn't a straight path. There are twists and turns, rerouting and backtracking. So to change things up a bit, this time, I thought it would be useful to hear more from readers and share their understanding of happiness, how it works and how we can all create more of it to enjoy higher quality of life. What you are about to read is a combination of the first book with fresh perspectives from readers and professionals in a variety of fields who have overcome obstacles yet continue to work on being inspired and motivated as part of their path to happiness. I hope you enjoy their wisdom and insights. And I hope you enjoy this little haiku:

KATHERINE GOTTHARDT

Inexplicably,
we still find happiness here:
Spring moon.

Here's to your journey, here's to finding your own spring moon!

Katherine

Questioning Happiness

Asking and answering questions is a classic method that supports learning and sharing new ideas. As a former community journalist and adult educator, I was comfortable with the approach. Want to gain new insights? Talk to people. Ask them about themselves, their lives, their experiences, what they think and why. Then listen to their answers. Truly listen, without interrupting, without judgment.

This can be a difficult process for the person asking the questions and the person answering. We're fortunate that members of the Get Happy, Dammit Facebook community offered to contribute their thoughts. They answered some important questions: How do you define happiness? What do you do to create more of it in your life? Got any tips? We're going to dive in, look at their responses, think about ways we can incorporate their ideas and see how we can build more happiness for ourselves and those around us.

One way to define an abstract is to make it concrete by using sensory images. It works because we are sensory creatures. We experience the world through taste, touch, sight, sound and smell. Our senses ground us and help us come to a different way of understanding what might be otherwise elusive. Traci Carrano Jones, Ph.D. illustrates this concept perfectly when she answered the question, "If happiness were an object, what would it look like?" Traci says:

> Happiness to me is being surrounded by feathers. These feathers cushion and protect from the harsh elements of the outside world. Happiness protects people from the outside world the same way feathers protect birds. I came to understand my definition of happiness through my struggles with life experiences and the knowledge I gained by incorporating the imagery of being surrounded by feathers as I traversed these struggles. It is a mindfulness concept. Being mindful of where I am and

knowing that "it is what it is" and that feathers protect me keeps me happy.

Reader Alexandra Mooney says, "Happiness is a family gathering together around a table to celebrate success and accomplishments of one another...filling the room with laughter, smiles, and even tears."

Grace Joy Reid offers a different visual:

> If [happiness] could be a living thing, then [it] would be an orange tree. This orange tree would grow the best tasting oranges in the world from the Western part of the U.S. When you bite into it, it would refresh, not just your palate, but also your entire being. You could have this special orange tree in your backyard. You would need to take good care of your tree (i.e., sunshine, pruning, watering, fertilizing and harvesting.). You would reap the harvest of all of your hard work by eating your fresh oranges, bringing you joy and fresh orange juice!

What great ways to explain what happiness means, how to grow it, how to experience it and even how to share it!

Grace's words inspired me to pen this short poem:

> *If happiness were an orange tree,*
> *would you pick a few fruits a day?*
> *Or would one or two suffice,*
> *each bite imparting lasting sweetness?*
> *Would you know how to nurture your treasure,*
> *when to water and prune it?*
> *Would you need to protect it from predators?*
> *Would the work be worth your while?*

GET HAPPIER, DAMMIT

Take a small bite of the orange.
Now tell us –
What are its ripest secrets?

Looking forward to next time,

Katherine

Get Inspired, Get Motivated

As a writer and educator, I've held many different jobs, unofficial motivator being one of them.

Let me tell you a sad story that took place many years ago at a postsecondary career school.

One day, the president tasked me to walk around and ask teachers and staff what motivated them, what inspired them. The goal was to collect positive quotes to hang on the wall of a new building. So off I went, pen and notebook in hand, goofy smile on my grown-up face, ready to hear from the area's best and brightest.

What I got was, "You don't want to ask me."

"I'm really busy. Can you come back later?"

"I'm seriously not the person you want to talk to."

"Excuse me. I need to grade these tests."

Now, I'm not here to be Suzie Sunshine. I know people have problems. I know life is not grand for everyone. I had plenty of problems myself, some of them pretty serious and life threatening. But when I looked around and saw how miserable so many people were, living in one of the wealthiest areas of the country — literally the land of opportunity with good jobs, homes and families — I had to wonder what was wrong. It wasn't just the job. It made me ask, why are we so beaten down? Where are our inspiration and motivation, the two things that make for a fulfilling life?

There are many reasons why we lose motivation and inspiration, but here's one that infects the brain, sometimes subconsciously.

Every day, we're bombarded with bad news. Whether from home, office or world, we face negativity at least hourly. That's a lot to manage. That's a lot to get past. That's a lot to let go of. So, in this book, I aim to overcome it, at least for a little while, and point out the positive. I'm not going to ignore the negative. But I'm not going to muck around in it. I'm going to process it and hopefully turn it into something better than it was at the onset. Here's why.

I value happiness. I value joy. I think they are worth fighting for.

Yes, I used the word "fighting" in referring to happiness and joy — because happiness and joy don't just happen. They come as a result of a positive mindset. How do you get a positive mindset? Motivation and inspiration. All of it takes work.

Mooney says, "Even though there are many challenges in life, I try to drive a path to happiness day by day, no matter if it is me having a fulfilling day at work, spending time to take care of myself, or spending time with those I love. It takes time and it takes patience with yourself and others to achieve happiness… Happiness comes in many forms, and will always come to those who strive for it."

So, let's start the work, shall we? I'll ask you the same thing I asked my colleagues many years ago.

What inspires you?

What motivates you?

What gets you out of bed in the morning?

What makes you proud?

It can be the smallest of things. Or is can be something you might have overlooked before. So, what if it is? Write it down. Say it. Share it. That's how you get more out of life. That's how you begin to make the world a happier place.

This morning,
car hood wearing
a slicker of pollen.
Even the rain
won't wash away
that yellow.
Quick, now.
Draw a heart in it.

In the spirit of self-discovery,

Katherine

Do the Work

You won't want to hear this. Building happiness takes work. But many people think, nah. "I don't want to 'work' on getting happier. If I have to work at it, then I'm not happy."

That's okay. Believing in the importance of building personal happiness isn't a moral mandate. What's interesting, however, is that the happiest people I run into have put effort into creating it. *Perhaps they didn't know at the time that what they were doing was building happiness.* But as they went on, they realized the results of their efforts were leading them in that direction.

Zach Tamer is one of these inspiring people whose life has become increasingly happy because of his efforts. Zach says, "Happiness is very important to me in my daily life. I would rate it as a 10 out of 10... I feel that if I am not happy, then my daily life suffers and if that unhappiness seeps into each day of my life, then my overall quality of life suffers, not only for me but for those around me."

This idea may resonate with you. So might Zach's journey.

Like most of us, Zach has not always had an easy life. He had to work at building his own happiness. But he also believes it's important work. Zach shares a little bit of his story:

> There was a time in my life when I was down on my luck, eating macaroni and cheese, hotdogs, and ramen for every meal for about six months. I had an apartment but didn't have any furniture and was sleeping on floor. I knew that just having that roof and having some food was more than some and that helped me to stay positive and understand the importance of having a roof over your head and food on the table. It also gave me a newfound appreciation for everything this world holds.
>
> I also spent much of my time during that six-month period standing outside at 5 a.m. hoping to get picked up by one of the trucks that came by looking for day la-

bor. Each morning was spent with people from all walks of life, from different parts of the world, who had different world views and experiences. Those mornings taught me a lot about humanity and that experiences, communication and sharing life's experiences with others, good and bad, brought me happiness.

Zach has turned his experiences into something positive. Not only has he built a happier life, but as a writer giving back to the community, he creates greater happiness for others, too.

Zach is a role model for those who believe nurturing happiness is possible and important. So assuming you do want to grow happiness in your own life (and have it spill into the lives of others!) what do you do?

First, answer these questions as honestly as you can. How important is happiness to you? And if it is important, how much conscious effort are you willing to put into building it?

There is no wrong answer to these questions. But if you do want to consciously create more happiness in your own life, I'd suggest moving on to these next questions: How do you define happiness? Is it a fleeting feeling? Is it long-lasting contentment? Something else? And what drives you? What brings you feelings of satisfaction?

Mooney says she came to her own understanding of happiness over time, through appreciating family and focusing on gratitude: "…by a man not just taking in my mother, but also me and my sister into his family out of love. Despite us not being related by blood, he raised us as his own. His sisters, brother, mother and father loved us and took us in without hesitation and made us whole."

Answering the questions that help you define happiness will take time and reflection. What you answer today might not be what you answer later – in the day, in the week, in the year, in the decade. This is why building personal happiness is a journey. As Zach demonstrates, it's not always an easy one, either. But if you believe in its importance, the work is satisfying.

> *That garden you decided to plant?*
>   *How it took time to turn over the soil,*
>   *get past the sweat, that insistent dust*
> *settling on your white sneakers. You cussed.*
> *Later you'd take that first bite of cucumber,*
>   *squirting refreshment from summer rains,*
> *several thick slices inviting another serving.*
>   *It felt a little like happiness.*

Here's to some moderately heavy lifting!

Katherine

A Rose Isn't Always a Rose

Ever read *Romeo and Juliet*? In a famous dialogue that people misquote all the time, Juliet says of and to Romeo:

> What's in a name? That which we call a rose
> By any other name would smell as sweet.

That's lovely, Juliet, but really. You're the Elizabethan emo kid who offed yourself for a boy-man. Should we really be building a philosophy around you?

I say that only half-joking. Let's take a closer look at what we had to read in high school. It's changed a lot since I was a kid, of course. We read Steinbeck and Hemingway and Plath, *The Great Gatsby* and *Anne Frank: The Diary of a Young Girl*. Everyone dies or kills themselves either in the stories or real life. Kids tell me it's not so different now, in terms of what they have to read in high school. I came out of high school believing I couldn't write unless I was depressed.

Think about this. You're young and hormonal. You're dealing with everything teens have to deal with just growing up. Then you are told to immerse yourself in horrors that are beyond most adults' ability to cope with — usually without much context or support.

Now before anyone gets the idea that I'm a book burner, anti-education, anti-reality, or anti-anything, stop. Just stop. That's not where I'm going with this. Where I'm going is here.

Words matter.

See, Juliet thinks a rose is a rose is a rose. The fact is, if you called a rose a turd, it would take on a totally different connotation. Before long, it would even stop smelling sweet, because words have the power to shape ideas. Words can spur emotion and action. Your mind largely believes what you tell it to, and we largely use words, even if we're not saying them out loud.

This doesn't mean we stop reading the hard stuff. It means we give it context. And we offset it with words that are empowering, motivating and inspiring. We intentionally feed our brains something other than gloom and doom, and we repeat those words in our head. We program ourselves to be more positive. You can attribute this phenomenon to psychology, neurology, linguistics, neurolinguistics — you can study it any way you want. Brain sciences confirm you have to be careful what words you put into your brain and when.

Writer Dottie Ward-Wimmer who describes herself as a "lover of life" says, "A dear friend who suffered mightily from depression would say, 'Today I will participate in my own happiness.' I think motivation may be akin to that." And it is, if you feed your brain the right words.

Here is another activity to try if you want to be inspired and motivated:

1. Read things that are inspiring and motivating.
2. Let the letters and words seep into your brain.
3. Read them out loud if you want. Or read silently, moving your lips.
4. Listen to the voice in your head. Let the voice read LOUDLY so you can hear the words.

> *Oh Juliet, I'm sorry—*
> *you got it wrong.*
> *A rose is a rose*
> *because we call it so.*
> *Call it thunder,*
> *and we hear the storm.*
> *Call it onion soup,*
> *and we smell the pungent kitchen.*
> *Call it the edge of a knife*
> *and we feel it touch the tenderness*
> *that is our skin.*
> *Feel how it pricks the forearm,*

drawing blood?
That's mortality leaking out.
Put your sword away.
Stand down.
This is my day.
You don't belong here.

Sending you all the right words,

Katherine

What do You Need?

Remember the chapter where I mentioned that "asking and answering questions is a classic method that supports learning and sharing new ideas"? Today we continue our series that examines happiness, how we can get happier, and how inspiration and motivation play important parts in the journey. In this installment, writer Derek Kannemeyer answers questions on what we NEED in order to be happy.

Needs as Motivators

As a species, we are enmeshed in our needs, from the bare-boned basics of food and water to what we believe is essential – whether it's true or not. Maslow's famous hierarchy of needs examines how humans are motivated by needs. He labeled needs from the physical to the quasi-spiritual, levels like physiological (food, water, etc.), safety, belonging and love, esteem and self-actualization. These needs motivate our behavior. And every time we move to another level, we are motivated to act in some way.

So what does this have to do with getting happier?

We are all in search of happiness in some way, and what we need plays into that search. Referring to basic needs, Kannemeyer says, "When a simple, genuine need is met: we're well fed; we're loved; we're rested; we have a nice cozy place we can call our own; the world about us is rich in serenity, or beauty, or liveliness, or strangeness," then happiness is easier to achieve.

Conversely, then, when our basic needs are not met, it's harder for us to experience happiness because we fall into self-preservation mode. In this frame of mind, we rarely have time or space to consider things like happiness. We are largely motivated to focus on survival. Kannemeyer says:

> When we're unfed, unloved, unrested, unsheltered, etc., etc.; when things are going wrong in our lives, and we

have no tranquility, and our bodies are broken, happiness becomes more fragile. And yet, more temporarily, any one of those *other* things going *right* will *still* make us happy!

He then takes it further, moving up Maslow's hierarchy, talking about how inspiration can also bring happiness through creativity. This is how happiness is built when more cognitive and spiritual needs are met. Kannemeyer says:

> When our curiosity is piqued, and our minds are engaged in acts of discovery and mastery; when our bodies are humming machines discovering what they're capable of and mastering *that*; when we make—create—even just fix something, something that's fully signed with our spirit...any and all of those can and will trigger happiness.

It's a lovely way of expressing those often-overlooked pathways to happiness, isn't it?

So now, I'll challenge you to examine your own needs. Are they being met? If not, how can you take action? Look at Maslow's chart, if it helps. Write down what you need from each level. Then make a plan, starting from the bottom up. Step by step, day by day, when you work toward meeting those needs, you will find yourself more motivated, more inspired – and happier.

> *Your whole soul grumbling*
> *like a long-starving stomach.*
> *What is it you need?*

Towards discovering our needs,

Katherine

Uncovering and Nurturing the Seeds of Happiness

"How can you be happy at a time like this?"

If you've ever been asked that question, you know what it's like to be judged for pursuing the positive, for seeking light in the darkness. It's common, and a lot of times, it's hard to understand. Where is this coming from, this "misery loves company" attitude?

It's coming, in part, from a focus on the negative, making us miserable and resenting people who have a positive attitude, especially during a crisis. There's actually a reason for it, too. With so much unhappiness making the rounds, positive people can be perceived as annoying. We become suspicious, like they are trivializing hardship. However, truly positive people aren't ignoring the negative. They are choosing to focus on the good they can control.

Yes, this is about control. When someone tells you that you have the power to make yourself happier, they aren't saying you have the power to overcome all that is wrong in the world. They aren't saying it's your fault you are unhappy. And they aren't saying you're wrong to be unhappy. What they are saying is, if you choose to and you want to, you can change your outlook, even if just a bit. And while it might not happen right away, you can start now by controlling what is in your power, by changing your focus.

One reader says about choosing to change his focus:

> There's a big difference between working on being happy and what people call 'toxic positivity.' If you look at what toxic positivity is, you find there's a lot of denial happening. A lot of shaming. Building happiness isn't like that. You aren't denying the world can be a hellish place to live in. You aren't denying your feelings or blaming yourself for feeling bad. You're simply

trying to do something to make your life better. It's about selfcare.

It can even be hard to get yourself to a point where you believe this, but once you are open to the possibilities, you are ready to give refocusing a try. Here's an exercise I've seen work time and again:

1. Find a peaceful place in your home or outdoors. It doesn't matter which, and it doesn't have to be perfect. It just has to be a place that brings you some kind of comfort.
2. Get into a relaxed position. It doesn't really matter what that is. Relaxation is different for different people.
3. Now, look around. Find one object that is pleasant to look at and focus on it.*
4. Look even more closely at the object. Notice the details, the angles, colors, texture. Pick it up, touch it, examine it.
5. Now think of how you feel when you feel something positive, like joy. Remember the feeling. You don't have to feel anything positive right now. Just think about how it feels.
6. When you think about that positive feeling, look closely again at the object as you hold it.
7. Do this for as long as you can concentrate.
8. Carry the object with you or put it in a place where you see it often. Pick up throughout the day.
9. Repeat these steps at least once daily as necessary.

*If you are visually impaired, you might try focusing on smell.

Here's why it works. By pairing an object with an emotion, you're creating an association. And by consistently reminding yourself of that association, you're changing your focus. It's simple, it's powerful and it's in your control.

We all know the world can be harsh and that we are living in times that make happiness feel more elusive. Do what you can to preserve the positive. It really is lying dormant inside you, waiting to be reawakened.

Early spring in the garden,
fingers in cool, moist soil,
I uncover the seeds
from last year's bloom.
There they are,
intact.

Until next time,

Katherine

Learning to Speak in the Positive

Which is easier, starting or stopping? It depends on the driver and the vehicle, right? There's also the angle, the incline and just plain gravity to consider. OK, stay with me.

We've been talking about how to keep motivation and inspiration going and some of the ways we might lose these critical elements of living a fulfilling life. We talked about what gets you up in the morning, how what you read and put into your brain affects how well you maintain motivation and inspiration.

Now let's talk about one kind of motivation in particular — the kind that helps us reach goals.

What comes to mind? Sweaty athletes? Some demanding voice in the background half-shouting, "You must believe in your dreams?" Sylvester Stalone? Maybe not. Maybe you think about tasks and checklists or quitting smoking or losing weight. How do you keep motivated to make that — or anything — happen? Assuming you've set reasonable goals, positive statements and affirmations can help.

Emphasis. On. The. Positive.

Here's why.

The brain recognizes positive statements, says Manassas-based hypnotherapist and educator Tim Horn. Social scientists, linguists and language-development experts agree. The mind tends to ignore negative commands, sentences and phrases that say what NOT to do. In fact, if you tell yourself, "Don't give up," your brain could do one of three things:

1. It disregards the negative command and does the opposite. So instead of hearing "Don't give up," it hears, "Give up." Not very useful, right?
2. The negative statement triggers rebellion, so you do the opposite of what was commanded. "Screw you, voices. I'm giving up."

3. Your mind becomes confused, not knowing which words to focus on, so your motivation and behavior become erratic or inconsistent.

If you want proof that what I'm saying is true, think back to a time when you've tried to stop or quit something. "I'm not going to eat chocolate anymore." The next day, you find yourself daydreaming about chocolate. The next day after that, you give in and chow down. Why?

Your brain focused on chocolate, Horn would tell you. It didn't hear "not." It heard, "yummy stuff of the gods." Chocolate took the wheel and drove you off a bridge into a fudgy ocean of cocoa addiction. So, you gave in, ate the chocolate and then flogged yourself for having no will power.

The thing is, it wasn't about will power. It was about words.

What if instead of focusing on chocolate, you asked yourself when you were most likely to eat chocolate? What if you discovered it was when you were tired? Great! Then you say, "When I'm tired, I'll take a power nap." No mention of chocolate needed, right? You follow the positive command: You nap instead of eating chocolate, you feel rested and you feel like you've taken a step toward your larger goal.

- It's not "I won't smoke anymore." It's something like, "When I feel the urge to smoke, I'll chew gum and squeeze my favorite stress ball."
- It's not "I won't yell at my children when they do the wrong thing." It's "I correct my children calmly and teach them how to do the right thing."
- It's not "I won't shop when I don't need something." It's "When I want to shop but I don't need anything, I make lists of things I already have."

See how it works? Well done! You've put yourself in the driver's seat. You have control. Now you've set yourself up for a positive spiral that keeps motivation going. "I did great yesterday. I know today I'll do great, too!" That's inspiring! And all because you used the right words.

> *Under the bridge,*
> *(in the dim and din)*
> *the wrong words sound right,*
> *blurred creatures of night.*
>
> *Drive the car down,*
>   *around the winding utility road.*
> *Park. Flick on the high beams.*
>   *Watch them*
> *scatter.*

Sending you all the right words,

Katherine

What Are You Really Looking For?

Most of us want to be happy. We have different ways of getting there, but at the base of it, enjoying life at some level is just plain attractive. Now, there are those folks out there who seem to thrive on maintaining their own misery. I'm leaving them out of the discussion, because I don't think they are the norm. (And some of them, even though they act like they love being miserable, really don't. They just think they don't have other choices.)

Getting and staying inspired and motivated is one route to happiness.

But how? The world can be a crappy place. There are social ills and war and nightmares beyond our imagination, some of them happening right in our backyards.

Let me tell you a story I heard a long time ago that I never forgot. I don't even know where I heard it, but I know it was said to be a true story of a Holocaust survivor.

A Jewish mother and her baby had been carted off in a train, destination Auschwitz. Now picture that. You're young, you have an infant you love and need to care for, and you're shoved into a cattle car. You only know where you're going can't be good. She arrives to suffer all the horrors that we hear about — torture, humiliation, death, all of it surrounding her. Her baby cries and is murdered in an unthinkable way. She's in utter darkness in every sense of the word. And then one day, she finds a random flower petal on the ground in the camp. Just one, white, thin petal, probably from a wildflower. It has been trampled on, but it's still fresh. She picks it up and puts it in her pocket. She touches it every day. She puts it in her mouth at one point and sucks the flavor of the flower right out of it. Then she puts it back in her pocket. And that's what keeps her alive.

Not possible, you think? It is if you're focused on the petal, and that petal has meaning. It is if you're grateful for a speck of beauty even amidst the ugliness. It is if you can believe that even in the darkness, there is a flicker of light waiting for you to notice. That's what the story was all about — finding hope, no matter how seemingly odd or scant. And that little hope provided the woman enough motivation to survive.

It doesn't get much worse than what that woman went through. Call it faith, God, Spirit, luck, chance, fate, absurdity — it's the little things that can keep us motivated enough to keep going. But we must look for them and focus on them.

Dottie Ward-Wimmer says, "Happiness lives all around us lives a constant sometimes silent, sometimes noisy hummmmm....BUT....we have to have the courage to listen... to embrace it... to let it in and live it."

Try this:

1. Look to your right.
2. Find the most attractive object within your grasp, no matter what it is. Depending on what's available, it might be something seemingly mundane like an interesting speck of dust.
3. Pick up the object. Look at it very closely until you notice things you never would have noticed before. Maybe that dust speck resembles something else. Maybe it's an interesting color. Maybe it's sticky or can float.
4. Write those attributes down. What do those things mean at a different level? For example, if your dust speck can float, what does that mean about the dust speck? About life?
5. When the daily grind gets to be too much, try to remember those things and/or repeat the exercise.

If you want to be happier, seek out and focus on the right things, those things that work in favor of motivation and inspiration. It's not going to be easy. You will need help along the way. Do the work. Accept the help. And when you're in a better place, be the one to offer help. You never know when you might be that petal, no matter your own condition.

> *These stories—*
> *which of these*
> *bring us to our knees,*
> *which to our feet,*
> *standing on tippy toes,*
> *stretching toward the sun?*
> *Those are the ones*
> *to read.*
> *To remember.*
> *Remember.*

Remembering the things that matter,

Katherine

Waking Up Is Hard To Do

Snooze is a funny word. Say it out loud. Look at it. Who came up with such a strange word for lightly sleeping? Dictionaries say unknown origin, maybe related to the sound of "snore." Snooze, snore — is that how you're getting through life?

I'm not one to judge. I often snooze on the couch, even for a few moments. I don't sleep as well as I used to. Everything hurts. Everything itches. Everything is just not right. Ever feel that way about life, that everything is an annoying itch or just plain painful?

I think it's normal from time to time. Okay. Set the timer. Take a nap. Ugh. It went off already? That means I have to get back to work. Quick. Hit the snooze button again.

Is this how you're living your life, physically or metaphorically? If so, you know already what it can do to your inspiration and motivation. Sure, sleep is essential if you want to be able to tune in to the gods or the muse or the birds or whatever speaks to you. And truth be told, what gets you out of bed might be something like the kids fighting or the dog whining. Or maybe you sleep well but wake up tired and say, "Bloody hell! I'm late ... again!"

Oh, the agony of waking up sometimes. It's no wonder you keep hitting the snooze button. But that's actually really bad for your brain, say the experts. You think you're getting extra sleep, but you're not. There's not enough time between alarms for you to slip into REM and stay there. You're just wasting time. And you're probably making yourself late and stressing yourself out as a result. Or the kids are going to start strangling each other or the dog is about to pee on the floor. Better to motivate yourself to get up and live your best day.

Here's what you can do instead of hitting the snooze button. Warning: It involves reminding yourself of your higher purpose in life — your "why" for living or doing your best (or even your why for reading this book). Try this, even if it's just for 10 seconds:

1. Open your eyes and stare at something. Anything. Re-orient yourself to the real world.
2. Think of what you need to do, the thing you're dreading, the thing you're avoiding. (It could be something as simple as getting in the shower.)
3. Now think of your higher purpose. That's right. Make that leap and do it fast.
4. What? Don't believe you have a higher purpose? Don't know what it is? Well, then you've got some work to do. Ask yourself why you don't believe or don't know.
5. By this time, you're either A, in an existential quandary, in which case your mind is far more alert or B, motivated enough to jump or roll out of bed. Either way, you're in better shape for getting up.

See? Instead of snoozing, you fed yourself a quick breakfast of motivation and inspiration. And that will be reflected in the work you do and how you do it.

Remember, hitting snooze is just a crappy coping mechanism. No one really wants to go through life every day, longing to get back to bed. While sleep is necessary and good sleep feels good, sleep isn't the higher purpose, the thing itself. So, don't keep hitting snooze.

Funny how flat the button,
so easy to lay a finger on,
and with the lightest touch,
lose moments of our lives.
What if we never hit snooze?
Good morning.

Wishing you wakefulness,

Katherine

Quit Messing Around

That's what I tell myself when I want to procrastinate (which is too often). Quit messing around. Well, sometimes I use stronger language, but this is a family publication. It's enough for you to know I give myself a stern talking-to, and then I sit down and do the hard work.

See, like most people, I can't afford to wait until inspiration and motivation waft in like some fabled specter. This isn't a Charles Dickens novel. Messenger ghosts and visions of dead bosses don't suddenly appear, tap me on the shoulder and say, "Write, oh bard! Write!" No. Like everyone, I've got deadlines. And sometimes, I've got deadlines to write about inspiration and motivation when I have neither. But here's one thing I've discovered about those two elements that make life so worth living: Doing something and doing it well inspires and motivates me.

That's right. The work itself motivates me, no matter what the work. I get a kick out of seeing that I've accomplished something and it makes me want to do it again.

Here's how to make that happen for yourself:

1. Close your eyes. Remember how good it felt to complete a difficult project in the past. Let that feeling seep into your skin. Revel in it.
2. Open your eyes. Make a list of things you need to do to complete the current task.
3. Work in 20- or 30-minute increments and start crossing items off that list.
4. Every time you cross something off the list, put a smiley face next to it, pat yourself on the back or tell your dog, "I did it!"
5. Repeat until the job is done.

Now, here's why it works.

First, remember we said whenever you connect the senses to something abstract, it becomes less abstract. So, when you allow a good feeling to overtake your whole body and you associate it with a memory, you ingrain that into your psyche, and you want more of it.

Then there's writing down your list. This is basically short-term goal setting, cementing each small goal kinesthetically by holding pen to paper and forming words. You can meet those goals if you know you aren't going to get overwhelmed. Short bursts of work are usually doable, which is why 20 or 30-minute sessions work. Move yourself through a few of those and reward yourself with a "Great job!" By the time you get through the process, you're ready to go back to the first step and integrate that wonderful feeling, which ... yes — gives you the motivation and inspiration to keep going. Before long, you're working in longer spurts because crossing tasks off that list is so damn satisfying. And sometimes by then, you're even enjoying the work itself.

This might seem like a pretty basic process, but it's one that has worked for me for decades. Turns out, the process is solidly based in education and psychology, too. And it can be applied to just about anything, making you more productive and leaving you feeling better about the work you've been putting off. One marketing professional says about this process:

> I have ADHD, so getting things done on a deadline can be a real challenge. Getting myself to focus....ugh! The lack of focus saps my motivation to do anything, and I want to just go to bed and pull the covers over my head. But if I can get myself to remember how it felt to accomplish something and take that first step to do it again, it's a positive spiral for me. Before I know it, I'm engaged with what I'm doing and I keep going.

Now to be transparent, I wasn't planning to share my trade secret when I sat down to write this chapter. It just kind of happened, and I don't regret it. I started off struggling, I went through the process, I got inspired and poof. Seemed like the right thing to do, so I did it. And it feels good. So, I'll probably knock out the next little bit, too. But first, a short poem.

> *Some days*
> *I wish for a specter,*
> *the ghost of Christmas past, perhaps,*
> *to remind me of better mornings.*
> *See how he carries me in from the cold,*
> *sets me softly down,*
> *points to the gift?*
> *Look at that red ribbon.*
> *How will I untie it,*
> *when all I can think of*
> *is dreaming?*
> *Enough, he tells me.*
> *Wake up!*
> *Run your fingers*
> *across the shiny surface.*
>   *Inhale the care*
>   *it took to create.*
> *Absorb the effort*
> *it required to wrap*
> *a masterpiece.*
> *Understand it was for you!*
> *Place the bow's end*
> *between finger and thumb.*
> *Hold fast, now.*
> *You're almost there.*

Sending you thoughts of productivity,

Katherine

What Is It You Need to Hear?

There's a Facebook meme out there that says something like, "For whoever needs to hear this ... your laundry needs to be put in the dryer."

This usually makes me laugh because I'm the last person who needs a reminder. You should see the pile in my family room right now. That's enough of a reminder for me. But I do often wonder what people need to hear and when. I know in my own life, I've run across an article or a song or a few words that were just what the doctor ordered — words that motivated or inspired me to keep going or to take action, words that helped keep me from feeling blah or numb to the beauty of life, in all its complexities.

The problem is those words aren't always around when we need them. The skies don't always open up the way we'd like and lead us to the rainbow's end. I'm not trying to kill the myth of the leprechaun or anything, but if that pot of gold really was there for taking, don't you think someone would have taken it already? Personally, I'd rather not wait to be hit on the head with the mallet of inspiration. When I need inspiration, I am motivated to go after it or create it. And that motivates me even more.

Want in? Here are a few ideas to get your head where you want it to be. You don't necessarily have to do them in public.

1. Sing the first song you ever learned as a child. I mean SING IT. Loudly. (It's okay to slur through the words you're not sure of.)
2. Look around you. Note five interesting or attractive objects. Describe them out loud.
3. Sniff the air. What do you smell? Acknowledge it. Out loud.
4. What's by your right elbow? Touch it. How did it get there? Recite the whole process.

5. What does the inside of your mouth taste like right this moment? Why? Verbally explain it to yourself.

What I just suggested you do is an auditory exercise based on all the five senses: sound, sight, smell, touch, taste, with an emphasis on sound. It goes back to what I said about the senses and humans being sensory creatures. We consistently forget what we are. We think we can live in our heads or on our computers. And while that's true up to a point, if we don't get back to our basic human components, those rooted in the senses, we lose touch with what it means to be human. And there's nothing that will kill motivation and inspiration more than that. Because no matter how much we might be loath to admit it sometimes, we are indeed human, and humans connect and perceive through the senses. It's how we build perception and meaning. It's how the brain works.

Now that you understand the concept, focus on what you need to hear. Whether it's through the car stereo or sounds you make yourself, feed your physical and metaphorical ears with the right stuff. Tired? Listen to something energetic. Bored? Listen to a TED Talk. Nervous? Shout out a short speech. No matter what you choose, make sure it's something positive, something that will support motivation and inspiration.

GET HAPPIER, DAMMIT

*Nothing sings so loudly
as the song of self,
the one with the words I learned
before I was even born.
Do you hear what I hear?
I think that might be my mother.
She birthed me with her music,
her low hum caressing my heart,
pushing me gently into a physical world,
reverberating with possibility.
How wonderful it is
to be human.*

Sending you the sounds of success,

Katherine

More Than a Gentle Nudge

My parents used to say about people who weren't motivated to do something necessary, "They're fine. They just need a kick in the pants."

That was the censored version, the one my mom demanded. My dad had other ways to say it that she didn't approve of. We grew up with a certain amount of acceptable censorship, because my mother didn't want us "talking vulgar." Except we lived in Massachusetts, so it was "vulgah."

"Mom, is 'butt' a bad word?"

"Kathy, don't be vulgah."

So "pants" it was. Never mind that it seemed to be OK to kick someone. Life is full of contradictions.

Eventually, I settled into my independence and into speaking the way I felt most comfortable — which was often vulgah. I don't think I thought too much about self-censoring until I had kids. That's when I quickly learned I didn't want my kids to use the words that I was taught were disrespectful, so I edited my words, at least until they were adults. At this stage in life, I've reached a comfortable, happy medium, somewhere between both my parents' versions of acceptable diction.

What motivates you to make life changes, or at least try?

For some changes, the motivation might seem obvious. "I want to lose weight so I can be healthier." Or, "I want to change jobs so I can earn more money." But what about the more complex things, the not-so-obvious, the quiet, underlying cause of action? What is really kicking you in the pants?

To get to these deeper answers, I suggest an activity I used to have my students do. I call it the Why Circle.

The premise is simple. You know how little kids ask "why" about everything? You do something similar. You keep asking "why" like a little kid until you get to a place where all the answers come back to the one before, in a circular manner.

Here's an example:

You say you want to change jobs to make more money.
Why?
I want to afford more of the things I like.
Why?
They make me happy.
Why?
They make me feel free.
Why?
Because I don't feel trapped.
Why?
Because I'm not poor and being poor makes me feel trapped.
Why?
Because when I was little, we were poor, and we were stuck in a bad neighborhood.
Why?
Because my parents couldn't get good jobs that paid enough.

You see how this works? You're digging to the very essence of your motivation now, the real reason behind what propels you.

Why is this important to know?

Because when the going gets tough, you'll need something more solid to fall back on, something more than, "I want to make money," or "I want to wear a little black dress to the cocktail party." There's more to it than that. There's more to YOU than that. Figure out what it is, and you're more likely to stick to the path that gets you to your goals. Because in the end, even the most superficial among us are not truly superficial. One manager at an IT company says:

> My 'why' gets me up in the morning and gets me through the day. When I get overwhelmed with the little tasks that add up or the stupid office politics or the things that make the job feel senseless, I remember why

I chose to do it and the real impact I'm having on the people I work with and work for. That makes all the difference, and I can go on.

There's a reason behind what motivates you. Find what that is, and you'll find even more motivation. And that will inspire you to continue your journey.

What is that
against my back?
The flat palm
of a convincing breeze
that urges idle swings "Move!"
creaking old chains
in the empty playground.
Kinetic energy —
it makes the world go 'round.
There is no better way
to stay ungrounded.
    Okay. Now fly.

Wishing you the why,

Katherine

The Wind Knocked Out

Ever sit down to do something and suddenly feel a lack of inspiration? What is that, anyway? You had a great idea. You were excited and motivated. Then poof. Gone. It's like you got punched in the gut. Your breath is knocked out of you. There doesn't seem to be a particular reason why. It just kind of happens.

The keyword here is breath.

If you look at the history of the word inspiration, you'll see it dates back to the 1300s and refers to immediate influence by a god or gods that breathe into a mortal to motivate them to do something creative while guiding them along the way. Inspiration is the breath of life, physically, spiritually and emotionally. Artists thrive on it, but so do good leaders and those who want to control their own destinies. So, there's good reason why losing inspiration can feel like you just got sucker punched.

Here's how to get it back.

1. Get somewhere private, or at least where you feel a sense of privacy.
2. Lower or close your eyes.
3. Listen to yourself inhale and exhale.
4. Feel your stomach and chest as you inhale and exhale. You can do this by putting a hand on your upper abdomen or just focusing on that part of your body.
5. Breathe deeply and slowly in and out for 30-60 seconds, continuing to listen to your body. If other thoughts intrude, don't fight them, but dismiss them.
6. Visualize someone or something physically breathing into you. Feel the air they bring through your nose, throat and lungs.
7. Open your eyes, take a deep breath, exhale and do what it is you sat down to do. Don't wait. Just start.

Why does this work?

Many times, when we feel we've lost our inspiration, it's that we have suddenly shut ourselves in or down. Whenever we do this, our breathing goes to hell. We breathe too fast or not at all. It's almost like a kind of anxiety. "I can't do this. This won't come out the way I want. I suck." All those negative thoughts break in and trample on what should be one of our best creative moments. When that happens, we literally stop breathing correctly. This is a physical reaction to an emotional response, and one perpetuates the other. One executive says, "It's so important to take a step back, clear your mind and just breathe. Don't think, judge or get distracted by any of the things that clutter up the day. Just completely remove yourself for a bit so when you come back, you have a clear head and a better perspective. I do this several times a day."

I'm not saying this is the only way to bring inspiration back. But it is a quick, convenient path back to the right mindset. Certainly, if you have time and inclination to walk in the woods, mediate, or take a warm bath and those work for you, go for it. But at the heart of all those activities is breath. Don't forget that. You don't want to end up distracting yourself with other activities, or you could end up losing focus and procrastinating.

> *When it comes down to it,*
> *words are breath,*
> *lifegivers of the creative,*
> *the inhale and exhale of cool air*
> *through the nostrils,*
> *into the heart,*
> *the very stuff of heaven.*
> *Ask not from where the breeze flows.*
> *It doesn't matter.*
> *Feel it on your shoulders?*
> *It's turning you,*
> *facing you in the direction*
> *of the life you're making.*

GET HAPPIER, DAMMIT

*Let it run its soft fingers
across your skin.
Breathe.*

Sending you glorious breath,

Katherine

Poisoning the King

Let's talk about what happens when you're motivated by anger.

One day, a king invited his enemy to a banquet at his castle. "Let's make peace," he said. "Come and celebrate my eldest son's birthday with us."

His enemy agreed, not knowing if the king truly had intentions of making peace, but he figured it would be worth a try.

In actuality, the king intended to poison his enemy at the banquet and show his young son how enemies were to be dealt with.

As they sat at the table, the king poured drinks himself and directed the servants to pass them around in such a way that his enemy received the poisoned drink. When it came time to toast, the enemy stood up, raised his goblet and said, "A toast — to our newfound peace and to this boy who will be a man someday. Boy, give me your goblet. Let us drink from the same brew your father has poured for me. We will share our drinks just as our kingdoms will share peace."

The father, horrified, stood and said, "No. Share your drink with me instead, as the boy has not been part of our feud. Come, I insist."

"Noble king," said the enemy, "what a grand idea. I shall instead share it with both, to ensure peace now and for future generations."

The enemy then poured some of his poisoned drink into the boy's cup and the king's cup.

"A toast to peace!" cried the enemy, raising his goblet and smiling.

"To peace!" shouted the guests.

And that's where the story ends. You see, it doesn't matter whether the king or the boy or the enemy drank the poisoned drink. If they didn't all drink together, the enemy would become suspicious and remain untrusting, forever inhibiting true peace. If the king drank and died, the kingdom would fall into ruin. If the king said nothing and just pretended to drink, at the very least, his son would die. And if he admitted to poisoning the drink, war would surely ensue.

That's what anger does. While it might poison your enemy (real or imagined), it also poisons those you love and yourself. While you might not drop dead at a banquet table, you most certainly cannot live your best life if your motivations are rooted in anger.

I've heard more than once that anger is a secondary emotion, the result of combined, deeper emotions like fear mixed with hurt or hurt mixed with sadness. Anger is a manifestation of those emotions and the situations that caused them. Anger is a demonstration that whatever created the initial emotions has not been resolved.

In most instances, I've found this to be true. I've also found it to be true that if we nurture our anger and use it as motivation, that motivation can be powerful. But anger, by definition, is a negative. The Oxford dictionary says anger is "a strong feeling of annoyance, displeasure or hostility." Unless anger is addressed at its base level, the level of those underlying combinations of emotions, it remains a destructive force.

So how do you ensure anger doesn't kill you and those around you? William Golden who describes himself as a naturally happy person says, "Happiness is about acceptance and then choosing your own path forward. We need to accept that bad, wrong, hateful, spiteful and unthinking surrounds us in this world. We can react or we can ignore OR we can choose the most positive path forward and be a light whenever we can."

Writer and community leader Cindy Brookshire has a system. She says, "Resentment comes from something you think you didn't get in the past. Anger comes from something you think you're not getting now. Fear comes from something you think you're not going to get in the future. Deal with your feelings." She suggests doing this:

1. Write down your feelings.
2. Deal with them, even if you need help from someone else.
3. Write down the things that make you feel angry.
4. Burn the paper in something contained, like a fire pit.
5. Wipe your hands off. The anger is done.

As a positive follow-up Brookshire suggests doing this: Whatever issues made you angry, perform one positive action each day to alleviate those issues. For example, if poverty makes you angry, join a group that helps the homeless or hungry. If your kids make you angry, consider attending a family support group together. The goal is to offset the negative with a positive.

Once you do this and anger is no longer in the mix, you'll discover your motivations are a lot less muddy and you can get on with your life. You'll become happier, as will those around you. And as a result, you'll become inspired to continue that upward momentum toward the positive and reaching your goals. New doors will open, revelations will unfold and you will find yourself evolving.

> *I hand*
> *a goblet of poison*
> *to my grey enemy,*
> *his fingers quietly closing*
> *around the stone base,*
> *touching my own.*
> *How the chill runs through.*
> *"No, you take the first sip."*
> *And I, foolish,*
> *raise it to my lips,*
> *pretend to drink and swallow.*
> *"More," says my enemy.*
> *"You've not had enough.*
> *Pour it in like you mean it.*

GET HAPPIER, DAMMIT

*I'm sure you can get a refill.
Am I right?"*

In the spirit of resolution,

Katherine

Developing What Matters

Take a trip back to your young adulthood. Were you someone who wanted to stand out or fit in? Both? Maybe you took a winding path in the pursuit of discovering yourself or defining yourself. Whatever the route, it got you where you are today. But now that you're older, have you thought about what sets you apart? I'm going to argue that while we need to fit in, the ability to celebrate our uniqueness plays into staying motivated and inspired. Here's why.

People are social creatures, by nature and necessity. Human beings have expressed tribal mentalities since the dawn of time. And yet, there is something appealing about being different — not so different that you can't fit in when need be, but different enough to make others take pause and think.

When I was a teen, I did this by wearing black. My mother hated it. Then one day, I decided to dye my hair darker brown. Except it came out black. So now I was looking pretty radical compared to my former self. I went into class and this girl with a black mohawk saluted me, hand covered in a spiky glove. "I like your hair," she said. I smiled. Yet, I was a bit uneasy. Did I want to be what was then known as "punk?" Did I want to stand out like she did? Was I ready for that?

The short answer was no. My boyfriend said he didn't like the black, so I changed it back. Yes, I caved. But since I was already on the fence about it, I didn't think it made too much of a difference.

Looking back, I wonder what might have happened if I had delved further into my punk side. As I type right now, I am looking at the rings on each of my fingers. I'm thinking about the four earrings in each ear, the tattoos and the funky top. My look is still a little different, but what's more important is how I live my life and my values. In fact, it's no one thing that sets me apart. It's more the unique combination.

So, what about you? Are you ready to use this introspection as a tool for motivating and inspiring yourself to go further than you thought you could? Give it a try.

1. Write down 10 traits that you feel make up you. These can be anything from how you dress to what you profess.
2. Of these, choose three that are the most important, that have the most depth.
3. Of these three, choose two that you most appreciate about yourself.
4. Each day, do one thing to develop each of those traits.
5. Mark off each day that you do your development activity. See how long you can maintain the practice.
6. At the end of a month, look at the changes you've made and how you've developed in those areas of choice.
7. Pat yourself on the back.

Here's the why. When you identify the unique things about yourself that you love enough to invest time and energy into, you grow in those areas. Every day, you become stronger. And that makes you feel good. The more you feel good, the more rewarded you feel, the more time and energy you put into developing those traits. And before long, you'll see yourself excelling, going beyond even your own expectations. You'll see the combination of those traits morphing in ways you didn't expect, and you'll be celebrating that. And you won't stop because you'll be inspired to keep going.

The funny thing is, we do this kind of thing all the time, but we don't notice it because we usually do it for pure enjoyment. For example, you might love to take photos. So, you buy a nice camera and you practice. Before long, you become an expert. That's great. But what I'm suggesting is that you choose something deeper than a hobby or job, something beyond the obvious. It might not even be something you enjoy. Maybe you start volunteering a few hours per month at a nonprofit that helps alleviate an issue that bothers you. Maybe you start cleaning and redecorating a room in your home that has no personality. Ah. Now I've created work for you, right? It's OK. You'll discover the work is worth it, especially the more you reward yourself by feeling good and recognizing the unique combination that makes up you.

We hear a lot about getting back in touch with "the real you," about being authentic, about releasing the inner child screaming to get out. These are all important, but it's equally important to discern what parts of the "real you" are truly what you want to invest in. Discover them. Develop them. Love them. And watch as the inspired miracle of you grows larger than life.

> *Did you dye your hair,*
> *thinking it would change you?*
> *Forget what you see in the mirror.*
> *The image shatters too easily.*
> *Fix your eyes on what's behind*
> *the shiny surface.*
> *Feel your stomach as you inhale.*
> *See how each deep breath*
> *expands the chest?*
> *They gift us life.*
> *Making us mighty.*

Celebrating the real you,

Katherine

The Motivation of "No Way in Hell"

"There's no way in hell I'm going to do the same thing my parents did."

Whether you're a parent or not, a lot of people think and say this. It's not that we all had crappy parents. It's just easier to see the mistakes they made because they made them on us. No, I'm not playing the blame game. Most children can pretty much say the same thing because no parent is perfect. My point here is, when it comes to motivation, sometimes it's the "No way!" that gets us moving in the right direction.

Now wait a second, you say. A while back, we talked about how the mind only reads positive statements, that when we say, "Don't do this," the mind hears, "Do this!" So how can a negative motivate the positive?

It's simple. A negative experience can be the catalyst that pushes you in the direction of your goals. After that, strategic, positive statements like affirmations need to take over. But negativity, if harnessed correctly, can be turned into a positive force to be reckoned with.

Carrano Jones says:

> For me, negative experiences demonstrate to me where I don't want to continue to live. They generally are uncomfortable spaces of time in my life I don't want to revisit. I try to gain insight from them and learn how to navigate around the pitfalls that led me to those experiences so that I might have more peaceful and positive passes next time the circumstance comes up. This is not a failsafe. There will still be negative experiences in all our lives, but they are opportunities for learning and growth, and that is the light that I try to see them in.

Here's an example. When I was a kid, I went to a really strict private school for a few years. I must have had the meanest teacher alive, because she spent most of my eighth grade year belittling me, telling me how I wasn't anything like my older brother (whom she had taught before and apparently adored) and how I was a disappointment. Big blow to the self-esteem, right? OK, now it's decades later, and I have my own kids. I vow I will never, ever let my kids have a teacher like that. That's the negative.

The positive? I was more proactive. I listened to my kids. I observed some of their classes. I went to parent-teacher conferences. I wasn't a helicopter parent, but I checked in periodically to make sure everything was working well. And guess what? My kids made it through school without having the same issues I did. They had other issues (you can't make it through school without having at least a few), but they had good teachers.

So now, I'm going to ask you to dabble in the negative a bit. Just dip your toes into a couple of bad memories. We're not going to bathe in them or stay there. Just give yourself a reminder of something you don't ever want to happen again.

Now, in one sentence, write it down. For example, "I will never, ever let a boss get away with cursing at me."

OK. Now … what positive things might you try to help ensure that doesn't happen? Write three to four steps you will take. But use positive language and make a simple, realistic plan. For example:

1. I use professional language, so my boss knows that's one of my values.
2. I speak to my colleagues with respect to show my boss I treat others the way I want to be treated.
3. When I am angry, I communicate clearly and appropriately to my boss and anyone else around me to provide a model for the way in which I prefer to be spoken to.
4. If my boss is headed in the direction of cursing at me, I calmly and politely redirect the conversation.

See how we took a negative situation and made positive steps to change it? It's really not so difficult — in theory, that is. So why don't we do it more often?

- We forget to practice the behaviors we outlined.
- We fall back into old patterns, speaking in the negative instead of the positive.
- We're so accustomed to the negative that we get discouraged and start to feel doomed to a fate we didn't choose.

The fix for this is to repeat the exercise again and again. You know how they say it takes 21 days or so to create a new habit? This is what you're doing. If that means sitting down every day and writing the steps, then that's what it means. This is how you'll stay positively motivated. Yes, it will take effort. Yes, you will get discouraged. But keep at it. Believe in the process. It works.

What do you see when you ask,
"What if?"
when you look into the eyes of the possible,
the maybe,
the last hope
groping a forgotten face?
Write it down,
there, in notebook, or on napkin.
Now, there's a plan.
Ink has made it so.
You have made it so.
Look who approaches!
Success, wearing the smile
of a child,
my old friend.

Rejoicing in possibility,

Katherine

Your Own Way Out of the Rut

I recently took an online class in strategic thinking in which the instructor asks, "How do you make time for strategic thinking?" Her response was the same one exercise gurus, life coaches and business thought leaders tout: "Make time."

"Make time" isn't as simple as people make it out to be. It's not always about time management and discipline. It's more about priorities and your state of mind. Let's switch up the focus. When it comes to creating inspiration and motivation in your life, how dedicated are you? How badly do you want and need inspiration and motivation?

I'll argue that you can't have one without the other, because inspiration fuels motivation better than any catalyst I've ever encountered. I'll also argue that emotionally, we crave both inspiration and motivation if we want to live our best life and move beyond the priorities of survival. So we make the time to do the work. Many of us are blessed to be in a place where we can do that. Carrano Jones says about making time:

> I have not always been so positive. It has taken a lot of self-reflection and self-inventory. I have explored my thoughts and feelings, and I have conceptualized how my perceptions may have been interpreted by others who may have had different life experiences than I have. All this thinking has led me to my level of happiness.

Maybe you are taking time to read this because at some level, you crave inspiration and motivation. If so, congratulations. You've got an appetite for the stuff. *But what if you don't desire inspiration and motivation and wish you did?*

This happens to all of us at some point. Sometimes we call this being in a rut. It's almost like we have to get inspired and motivated to want more of it enough to make time to nurture it.

If you find yourself there, here are some simple things you can do:

- Go online and read inspirational quotes. Seriously. Even if they are lame.
    - Why? The messages seep in. (At the very least, you'll find something stupid to laugh at.)
- List three small, common things you are grateful for.
    - Why? Ruts are partially created from taking things for granted. When we do that, we overlook the importance of little blessings, and those can be inspiring.
- Go outside and look up. Examine the clouds or the stars, the birds or the planes. Appreciate them.
    - Why? When you re-establish the wonder you held as a child, you tend to get back to the basics of inspiration.
- Plop some paint on a piece of cardboard and swirl it around. Mix in some more colors. Watch how the colors merge and morph. If you feel the desire to finger paint, go for it.
    - Why? You're activating the creative side of your brain, fueling inspiration.
- If you have children or friends, no matter what the age, color or draw with them. Or write a silly poem using inane rhymes.
    - Why? Group creativity and fun foster an environment where inspiration can grow.
- Go for a short walk. Really note the details: the paint peeling on the fire hydrant, the colors of the wildflowers, the texture of the sidewalk.
    - Why? Being observant grounds us in the moment, makes us see things we ignore and brings new understanding, which is inspiring.

- Redecorate your office, even if you just switch out a couple of things or rearrange your desk.
  - Why? It forces you to be more observant and create positive change within your surroundings. And it could inspire you to do more after.
- Do something out of the norm, even if it's just saying hello to strangers.
  - Why? It helps disrupt the common and snap you out of your rut. And it makes you think of other ways you can make changes including … you guessed it. Making more time to nurture inspiration and motivation.

Artist Sima Button offers another path. She says, "Motivation and inspiration are like hygiene. You have to be consistent." She suggests, "Seek out good books, music and people. Surround yourself with inspiring works and people and visit them on the daily."

You might discover that after reading these suggestions, you say to yourself, "Bull. I know what inspires me. I'm going to do it." Great! Do what works for you. You know yourself and engaging in this inner argument will inspire you to understand yourself even more.

Carrano Jones would agree. She says: "I believe I have influenced others, but happiness only comes from within. I may have suggested things for others to think about which may have pointed out a direction for others to go on their journey, but ultimately everyone is on their own journey."

When you know what makes you tick, you will know how to fuel your inspiration and motivation.

> *They told me "Make the time,"*
> *but it felt like doing time,*
> *hash marking days on the wall,*
> *scraping my nails to the nub on cement,*
> *in the same prison that has bricked*

*unfortunates for ages uncounted.
Instead, I make the rhyme,
using the words in my mind
to meter out the obvious,
the mundane, the cell,
the overwhelming whiteness of it all.
Oh, how they lie,
how they lie.*

Offering the gift of time well spent,

Katherine

Putting Fleeting Moments on Pause

One weekend, I went on a little trip with my sister-in-law to the beach, and after, posted this on Facebook:

> Walking by the pier at Colonial Beach, Virginia and a gentleman in a wheelchair carrying fishing rods went past me and hooked my hair in one of the lures. So, there I am, following him so my head doesn't get ripped off, and people are telling him "Stop!" After a brief ruckus, a man comes over and helps unhook me. "I don't think I was what he was expecting to catch," I say. Then he asks if my SIL and I like ice cream, at which point his friend comes over and asks my SIL, "Who do you think Jesus is?" and does she want an ice cream coupon. So, then I'm thinking about them as being "fishers of men" but I'm kinda wondering how Jesus would feel about the whole ice cream bribe thing. I start looking around for a white van with no windows. Because that whole thing was bizarre. But it might make a great one-act play.

That ridiculous story got a lot of likes and laughs. And yet, it happened so quickly, and my sister-in-law and I didn't really laugh or talk too much about it. It was only later that I could see the humor and the value of that little incident. What was the value? It inspired me to write the post and now, this chapter. And who knows. Maybe I will write the play.

Sometimes the most fleeting things make for the best inspiration, motivating us to go with it and take it further. When we do that, we give those moments a life of their own. And we create lasting memories. We create meaning and purpose. If you've ever made a scrapbook or used a photo as the basis for art, you understand the concept firsthand. It's these snippets in time that hold more value in retrospect than we might have thought at the time they occurred.

Often, these brief occurrences live in our short-term memory, so if you want to harness them, you need to note them right away or they are easy to forget. Here are some ways you can keep track of those moments so you can return to them for inspiration when you want, while strengthening memory.

1. Carry a notebook or note-taking app and jot down simple happenings throughout the day. Use lots of verbs and descriptions to keep it vivid.
2. Take photos of little things that catch your eye. Maybe it's a weird bug on your front door or someone's colorful shirt.
3. Listen. Really listen. What do you hear around you? Record it if you can. If you can't, write it down. It might be something like ice from the ice maker falling into a container, the buzz of a toaster that burnt bread or a cat drinking water.
4. Go back and consider where you were when these things happened. How do they make you feel? Happy? Sad? Grateful?
5. What meaning do these moments hold for you? For example, I'll now always remember that trip to the beach I took with my sister-in-law and the talks we had while we were there.

Besides helping you live your best life, these practices are useful tools for creating art. Or you can use them in a class or workshop in just about any setting. Try them out and see the variety of applications. You'll probably discover that when you invest in fleeting moments, you'll get many fulfilling returns.

GET HAPPIER, DAMMIT

*Hooked on the fleeting,
I watched the jet ski fly by,
waves following,
like a memory.*

Slowing down the moments,

Katherine

Uninspiring, Unmotivating: Groupthink

Ever watch one of those post-apocalyptic movies where hoards gather and for whatever reason — be it hunger, fear or contagious bad attitudes — a fight breaks out and suddenly, it's mass chaos? Or how about a bar fight? Everyone jumps in and starts breaking chairs and bottles. Or maybe it's just a concert or sporting event, and the crowd goes wild over the performance. Nothing bad, they just do it together. All of these are examples of groupthink, which is based on behavior without critical thinking and reflection. Whether good, bad or indifferent, groupthink can be the nemesis of true inspiration and motivation. Here's why.

At its very heart, choosing to be inspired and motivated is a personal, thoughtful decision. So, it makes sense that when you allow a group to think for you and you just follow the crowd, you become less inspired and motivated, even if the crowd is doing something positive. How can that be?

1. Groupthink operates on collective behavior, which encourages sameness. However, we're all individuals, and if we let the group think for us, we give up our unique capacity to create the meaning behind inspiration and motivation.
2. Groupthink is typically transient. Get out of the group, and you're left alone with yourself and your thoughts. Now what? Do you know what to do with your mind? You might use memories to go back to the moment where you were part of the crowd, but that is inherently a solitary journey.
3. Groupthink tends to be shallow. Your quest to maintain inspiration and motivation is not. Thus, groupthink is at odds with your goals.

I know. No fun, right?

Actually, that's not true. You can use groupthink to your advantage, and as you do so, distinguish yourself from the group. It might not happen at the scene where collective behavior is taking part, but that doesn't matter. When it comes to working on creating your own inspiration and motivation, you can use the group, but you don't have to depend on it.

Here's how:

1. Break away mentally and/or physically from the group. Observe. Note the dynamics of the collective behavior and kind of thinking that is going on in the group. Feel free to jump back into the fray — unless you are in a barfight or a postapocalyptic brawl. Then you might want to leave.
2. Go back to the haven of your independent mind. Assess how the scene of the collective behavior made you feel (i.e., the bar, the sports arena, etc.).
3. Now assess how the idea behind the collective behavior made you feel. For example, why were you in the bar to begin with? What started the fight? Or what was the music about? Was there a history behind the sound and lyrics?
4. Jot down notes and consider how each of these can be used to inspire or motivate you.

It might look something like this:

> Went to the concert. People singing and dancing in unison. Loud drums. Fireworks. Smoke machine. I felt exhilarated being part of the crowd enjoying the music. It was freeing to be part of a group that was there for the sole purpose of celebrating the music. It felt peaceful and made me happy.
> I am inspired by the music.
> I have always wanted to sing.
> I'm inspired to practice and motivated to take lessons.

Notice the above thought processes. The ideas must form in your mind independently, and they can't do that in an environment where everyone is thinking the same thing — or not thinking at all and just acting on instinct.

I encourage you to think for yourself. So will others who respect your decision to work on your quality of life, personally and professionally. One manager at an IT company says, "I actually love when we're in a meeting and that one person says 'I don't think that will work' when everyone else says it will. That's the person I want to hear from because that person is thinking differently. I want to know what the outcomes of my decisions could be, the potential risks that others haven't considered. You can't get that if everyone is just nodding in agreement."

Whether it's the boardroom, the bar or the concert hall, the benefits of independent thinking outweigh the ease of groupthink. Take control of your thinking, and celebrate success when you do.

> *In the 80's,*
> *there,*
> *in row 103,*
> *me,*
> *lighter raised,*
> *like everyone else*
> *But mine –*
> *I make it dance for* me.

In the spirit of inspiration,

Katherine

Hanging With a New Crowd

You're not being realistic.

That's the response you might get when you decide to become more inspired and motivated, moving toward greater happiness in life. But you know what? That's okay, especially when you understand a little of what might be going on in other people's heads as you make positive changes.

The first thing to understand is that on a primitive level, humans are social creatures who have an underlying need to be accepted. Once you understand that, it's easier to understand other people's behavior and why they might think the way they do.

Many times, people who want to be accepted engage in negative groupthink. It's just easier to be negative, to steamroll over anything that keeps inspiration and motivation going, and it's even easier to do it when everyone else is. It's a negative spiral that reinforces itself and the people involved.

So how can we immerse ourselves in our efforts to be inspired and motivated when the crowd says it's better to be cynical, support the status quo or stick to negativity?

Let's be real. None of those things are going to make us happy. Sure, they might feel OK for a while, because they keep us in a certain ironic comfort zone. But that's not where you can stay if you want to get the most out of life. This means, that to be inspired and motivated, you might have to accept not being accepted.

Ouch, right? How can not being accepted possibly bring happiness? Isn't that a negative?

Don't worry. If you're doing this right, it shouldn't be as painful as it sounds.

Here's more on how it works.

You change

As you grow, these changes take place and you begin to gravitate toward those who are more positive. This increases your own success rate of becoming inspired and motivated, because you start spending more time among positive people. You also start to understand positive people better, and where in the past you might have mocked their sunny dispositions or have harbored jealousy over their genuine happiness, you appreciate their attitudes and approach to life. When you begin to accept them, you find yourself also being accepted, and you begin to attract more positive people. Soon, you will find you will be surrounded by positivity, with people who have goals similar to your own.

Other people change

When you dedicate yourself to becoming more inspired and motivated, you influence the people around you. They will see the changes in you, and they will usually either open their minds to what you are doing in your life, or they will gradually distance themselves. Both responses progress naturally and incrementally, and unless you have abruptly changed your behavior or are in a highly toxic environment, there generally won't be dramatic discord. The transition just kind of happens. People adjust.

The other good news is, the people who truly love you usually accept these changes, and many even appreciate them. They want you to be happy. And you become a beacon of hope that greater happiness is possible for them, too. One educator said about her process, "I learned that as family, we must love each other as we are in each moment, and that means accepting people change, just as we do. If we want others to accept our changes and the things we consider growth, we need to do the same for them. It's kind of the golden rule of living peacefully and happily."

Now that you know things are going to change, you'll need some basic change management techniques. Here's how you can help ease the transition as you align your mindset toward being inspired and motivated:

1. Communicate. Tell the people closest to you what you're trying to accomplish. Explain your why and your how. Explain that their friendship means something to you, which is why you want to share your thoughts on the changes you're making.
2. Speak about your experience naturally and with empathy, understanding this might be hard for them to understand or accept. Don't be preachy, pushy or condescending. Remember, you are choosing to grow your inspiration and motivation to better your own life. Others might choose a different path.
3. Invite those closest to you to join you in a way that makes sense. For example, if you're using a journal to write out your goals or take notes on the beauty around you, ask friends and family if they would like to journal with you. When you do this, explain the concept behind the activity and why you enjoy it.
4. Go gently. Avoid rapid, overly obvious behavioral changes. Those tend to be more superficial anyway, and you are looking to make lasting changes.
5. Don't judge. Remember, you might have been in a less happy place at one time, too. Stay away from trying to analyze why someone else might choose to work at something other than becoming inspired and motivated and focus on your own journey.

Change is not easy and getting others to accept the changes they see in you can seem daunting. But by using a strategic approach based in better understanding human behavior, you can make the changes you want to make and get the acceptance you need to be happy.

KATHERINE GOTTHARDT

How unhappy the worm,
eyeing a bird,
knowing it cannot fly –
unless ... Unless.

Wishing you gentle, positive change,

Katherine

It's Contagious

Inspiration is a social disease. So is motivation. It's amazing how when one person shares one or both, others catch it, like a virus. It's not the kind of virus you want to cure, either. In fact, most people would appreciate a sneeze in their general direction if you are spreading inspiration and motivation. As one coach said, "I'm not sure what you're carrying, but if you want to share it, I'm not going to complain."

Here's why inspiration and motivation can be contagious.

As we know, people are social creatures, even those who seem to prefer the hermitage. Humans have a fundamental longing to be with others. It's part of the survival drive. Statistically, we tend to live longer when we live harmoniously with fellow humans. And what happens when we live with others? We tend to influence one another's behavior and thinking. Now, that can be a bad thing in the case of groupthink, where you lose your identity and ability to independently analyze. But it can be a good thing if you're spreading something positive, like creative inspiration and motivation.

Have you ever been in an audience and listened to a story so compelling that the audience gave a standing ovation? Did it give you chills? Did you cry along with others? That was inspiration speaking.

Have you ever played in a band and intensified your performance because of what you saw and heard your band members doing? That was inspiration acting out.

How about teaching? Ever get that teaching high when speaking passionately about what you love and the class nods in understanding? That was inspiration listening.

What you want to do is get into situations where you catch that inspiration. To do that, you need to watch who you hang out with. Debbie Downer doesn't do it when it comes to giving you what you're seeking.

But let's talk about Debbie, shall we? Maybe what Debbie needs is for someone else to be inspired, someone else to spread that germ and lift her up. Once you have what you need, you might be in a position to do that. But first, make sure you've stocked up on your own inspiration. You don't want Debbie to bring you down.

Here are some ways you can find people to help inspire and motivate you:

1. Join a book club or start one that only reads inspirational books. Read the books. Discuss them. Let the discussion infuse you with inspiration and motivation to continue. Build off each other's inspirational high.
2. Attend a conference where you know motivational speakers will be addressing the crowd. Listen — really listen — to the experiences the speaker shares and see how you might apply their approach to your life. And if they're good, nod and give them that standing ovation.
3. Take in short, inspirational and motivational videos or podcasts online, but do it with a friend or two. Avoid trite videos that don't build on your current understanding of inspiration and motivation. Observe the audience. TED talks, for example, tend to be meatier and provide inspiration from some surprising people, ranging from artists to scientists.
4. Make lists of groups that inspire you. Or make a storyboard with photos of victorious people and quotes that have the same effect. Pin these to visible places. Look at them and read them every day. Share them with others. When you get bored with them, replace them with something new.
5. Sit in the park or another public place and people watch. Observe the people who seem like they are most enjoying themselves together. What are they doing? How are they interacting? Make a story in your mind about what motivated them to be there. What do you think inspires them? Can you relate?

Now what do you do with all this inspiration and motivation? You could:

- Start a new project.
- Finish an old project.
- Set new goals.
- Meet current goals.
- Share your inspiration and motivation with Debbie Downer.
- Let yourself fall in love with life.

People are complex. They can be catalysts for the negative or the positive. Surround yourself with inspiration and motivation and see how your own will bloom.

Watching wings
point to the sky,
I wonder how I ever
remained grounded
with swallows nearby.
If I touch their feathers,
will I, too, fly?

Motivating you,

Katherine

Who Are You Listening To?

"Just shut up!" Ever scream that in your head as someone is talking? Sure, you have. Sometimes we do it if we disagree with someone. But a lot of times it happens when someone is breaching our psyche with negativity.

I've mentioned before the importance of surrounding yourself with positive people. Now let's look a little more closely at those people and what makes them so powerful and important, what makes them worth listening to.

Probably the two most positive, strong role models I've ever had were my own mother and my husband's mother. And they could not have had more different personalities had they tried. What they had in common was the ability to find inspiration all around them and the ability to laugh.

My mother was a teacher's assistant. She taught me to read, and as soon as that happened, I began to write. But she wasn't educated herself. In fact, she never became a teacher, doubted her ability to learn new things and lived below the poverty line most of her life. Everything she had learned came from the Girl Scouts, church and experience. And still, the woman who told me in this aggravatingly optimistic tone as she was deathly ill, "It's OK. It's all part of life," made me understand that you could be happy living on next to nothing, you could inspire people who had it worse than you did and you could motivate people to get to the next level of personal development.

My mother-in-law, though she wasn't highly educated in the traditional sense, was always taking classes — painting and quilting, in particular. She read Wayne Dyer and believed in something bigger than herself, even though she said she didn't really know what it was. She didn't care that she didn't know. She was chatty, sarcastic, funny and giving. She had grown up in poverty and seen some seriously hard times. She'd give me no-nonsense, practical advice, talk to me for hours, teach me new skills and made me see that laughter was truly the best medicine for most things.

I've had some seriously negative people in my life, too. You can't get through life without encountering them, but who was I going to listen to? The people who eventually would drag me down with them if I let it happen, or the people who lifted me up?

Don't misunderstand. While I would never suggest anyone stay in an abusive relationship or a toxic environment, I recognize you can't cut negative people out of your life entirely. If you did, you'd be cutting out everyone because everyone is negative sometimes. But you have a choice. You can listen to the people who inspire and motivate you, or you can listen to people who make you feel like garbage. By garbage, I mean, they make you feel bad about yourself and/or the world around you. They suck the inspiration and motivation from you.

So how do you decide? I'm not going to tell you what to do here. It's not my place. But I'll tell you some of the ways I do it.

1. Simple math – If you make me feel bad about the world more than 20% of the time I'm around you, I'm out.
2. Small doses – If you're a negative person but I still like you for whatever reason, I'll put you in this bucket and be with you for short periods of time, but that's it.
3. Grain of salt – If you're an inspiration killer, I'll hear you out, but I won't internalize what you're saying. You'll get the "whatever" response from me (even if I don't say it).
4. Boundary building – If I have to work with you but you're unmotivating and uninspiring, I'll build a wall around myself and keep just a little window open so I can hear you.
5. Cutting out – If you're toxic or abusive, you have no place in my life.

You will have to decide how to handle the people who suck inspiration and motivation from you. Once you do that, you'll see it's a lot easier to do the fun things we've been talking about, like making storyboards of motivational people, taking photos to capture inspiring moments and setting goals for the future so you have something to look forward to. One manager working in food services said, "I know most people who really go off aren't that mad about their burger not being right. They're mad about something else that has nothing to do with me or my team. I've learned to wear a certain mental armor that lets me deal with difficult people in a professional way. It's how I protect my well-being. And after I have a negative interaction, I counter it by seeking out someone positive right away. Seriously, this keeps me sane."

So what's your plan for dealing with negative interactions? Take a moment to examine a situation and map how you'll continue to feed your motivation and inspiration in spite of them.

Search the crowd
from behind.
Whose head sits taller,
straighter, face forward,
as if thread from clouds
swaddle them in a white web,
enough to hold the two of you?
Grab a few strands.
Make a cradle.
Rest easy with them.

Focusing on the positive,

Katherine

Whatever It Takes

Do you feel like a dumpster fire? A train wreck? A catastrophe? Did you think being a grownup would magically make that disappear, as if age would remove that vulnerability you felt as a child? Were you disappointed to discover that wasn't the case? If all this resonates with you, congratulations. You're human. If not ... just wait. No life is without those moments that seem to dump you off a cliff into a raging ocean.

Here's the good news. Even if that ocean leads to a waterfall and you tumble into nothingness, eventually landing in churning water that seems impossible to survive, you're moving. And you're moving away from the waterfall, toward a different part of the story. Maybe you find a log and float for a while. Maybe you drag your beat-up body to the shore. Whatever happens, you've moved past the worst, and you've reached a quiet that gives you time to catch your breath and regroup.

When I worked in the classroom, I met students who had overcome odds I never could imagine facing. While my earlier life was not easy, these young people had seen the horrors of war, gang fighting, street culture, drug addiction, generational poverty and enough death to last them a lifetime before they had even hit their teens. Then one day, I asked them to think about what made it so they were able to sit in class and consider improving their lives — what motivated them.

One girl in her mid-20s raised her hand. She said, "To get here, I have to step over druggies in the hallway of my apartment building. I take the train in. It takes me two hours to get here. But I don't care. I'm the one supporting my whole family. I'll do whatever it takes."

For her, supporting her family motivated her to try to make a better life. It got her to school and work every day. It got her to graduate.

In an earlier section of this book, we talked about the why. Now, I'll challenge you to think about the how. What are you working toward? What does "whatever it takes" look like for you? And how will you stay motivated to do whatever it takes?

No matter where you are in your journey toward becoming more inspired and motivated, I would encourage you to do something we did as a group in class: brainstorm. It doesn't matter if the ideas seem simple or outlandish. It doesn't even matter if they are realistic. What matters is that you use your most creative energies to generate some hows. These form the inspired basics of a plan, one you can tweak to suit your personality and lifestyle later. But when you brainstorm the hows, you have the chance to pump yourself up, motivate yourself to ignore limitations, to use what you know and expand to beyond the possible. This is what visionaries do, and I'm asking you to be a visionary in your own life. Wimmer says, "Move...take a walk... sing out loud..... give yourself a hug and permission to be uninspired and, as you can, give that permission a time limit... after which you will allow yourself to be open to the possibility of inspiration."

Here's what brainstorming might look like for an overweight, overly stressed woman in menopause. (Oh, wait. That's me!)

> How will I get to where I want to be one year from now? What does "whatever it takes" look like?

- I'll run every day.
- I'll eat under 1000 calories per day.
- I'll eat more protein.
- I'll get weight loss surgery.
- I'll pause throughout the day to reduce my anxiety.
- I'll meditate.
- I'll check out hypnosis.
- I'll take a trip to a mountaintop in Tibet and speak to a guru.

- I'll buy a bike and ride it.
- I'll hike in the snow.
- I'll get a life coach.
- I'll trying counseling.
- I'll take time out for me every day.
- I'll go to the doctor to check out my hormones.
- I'll focus on self-care.

Okay, so as an overweight, menopausal women with bladder, back and knee problems, running is out at the moment. And a trip to Tibet is a bit costly, but someday, I might get there if I start saving money now. Pausing during the day? I can do that. Take time out for myself and focus on self-care? Go to the doctor? I can do that, too. Weight loss surgery? Extreme, but I have the ability to do it. And that will help me eat 1000 calories a day. Bike riding? Maybe after I lose some weight from hiking in the snow or weight loss surgery or both. Hypnosis, coaching and counseling? Throw those in. Every bit helps.

So now, I've narrowed down my list to something manageable and realistic. I won't entirely give up on the more elaborate dreams, but as I achieve my goal of becoming healthier, I will find that those dreams will change, too. In one year, when I'm healthier, I'll have different dreams, and I'll do the same exercise. It might be useful to keep this list and compare. How have I changed in one year, not just in terms of where I am with my health, but what my list looks like?

If I'm successful, have I done whatever it takes? Sure. See, whatever it takes doesn't have to be extreme. It's all about finding the how. The swim might be long, but you can make it out of the water one doggy paddle at a time.

Turns out the waterfall
*   dropped me*
into a deeper pool.

Who knew
I could hold my breath this long?
Look.
The shoreline.

Wishing you the best list ever,

Katherine

Rediscovering Your Core

Here's a piece of advice I've received more than once from different wise people at different points of my life: Get back to your core values.

These folks weren't moralizing. They were reminding me to remind myself who I am and who I want to be. Why? Because I had fallen into a period of sticky anxiety mixed with a heavy dose of meh — not good for anyone who thrives on feeling inspired and motivated to meet the next challenge. Heck, not good for anyone.

So, let's talk about core values and what they actually are by addressing what they aren't.

It's not about age

Your core values aren't necessarily the things you were told to believe as you were growing up. And they aren't necessarily the things you believed since you were young. See, core values don't have to do with age. Just because you learned something as a child doesn't mean it's correct, right? We believe lots of strange things when we're kids. As we grow, we shed some of those beliefs in exchange for new ones that reflect our adult experiences and understanding. I'm not saying that your core values must be different from those you held as a child. But know if they are different, that's okay.

For some people, this is hard to get past. We grow up believing authority figures are right, and it takes all our inner strength to question the validity of what we've been taught (which is why adolescence is typically so tumultuous). But if we don't question what we've been taught, how are we supposed to grow? And for our purposes, how are we supposed to set goals, reaching for more inspiration and motivation, if we're stunted or caught up in false beliefs about ourselves and the world around us?

Think of it like this. When we were babies, we ate baby food. But now, for the most part, we don't. Why? We need something with more substance. And while the base of the baby food might be similar to what we have now, the form is necessarily different. Some of that baby food might not even agree with us anymore. Maybe they don't taste good anymore. Maybe they are bad for us. We've had to figure out which foods to keep eating, which to stop. It should be the same for your core beliefs.

It's not about being bad
This is a hard one, too. Because we're taught to respect our elders and authority, when we realize we disagree with their assessments and change our core values, we often feel guilty. While this is a normal response to conditioning, we have to get past that if we want to progress.

Here's a little about my personal journey. I was raised in a strict Catholic family. For several years, I went to Catholic school. However, we also explored various churches that taught very different aspects of Catholicism, some considered liberal, some conservative. As I got into my teens, I started questioning everything I ever knew about what I'd been taught — which is normal. I began to explore other religions and beliefs. I dove into books and classes and visited other institutions of faith, some of which were quite different from my childhood churches. I realized my beliefs were a combination of those practiced in a variety of cultures and institutions. Slowly, I put together a list of my own beliefs based on these experiences.

Let me tell you, reading that list, even now, throws me into fits of inspiration. I feel more in touch with my spirituality, my sense of a higher power and my ability to live what I consider a good, moral life. And I'm motivated to practice my version of faith each day. And yet, as I grew into this practice, I felt guilty. My parents were disappointed in me because my spiritual journey didn't match theirs. It was something I had to do, though, because my core was different from theirs. But it was mine. I had to own it and live it if I wanted to do my best.

Everyone has a different way of developing core values and honoring them. Mooney speaks of her core values like this:

> Even though there are many challenges in life, I try to drive a path to success day by day, no matter if it is me having a fulfilling day at work, spending time to take care of myself, or spending time with those I love. It is very important in my life that the connection between me and those I love is maintained. Every bump in the road, failure and win, I share with my family.

When you figure out or reidentify your core values, you will discover they are, in some way, unique to you. However you decide to practice them will also be unique to you. And those practices might change over the years. You might even tweak your core values as you go along. All of this is okay, as long as you keep in touch with who you really are and what you believe. The more you do this, the more empowered you become. And that's both inspiring and motivating.

How do you get there? Try this, to start.

1. Write down three things you were taught to believe about yourself.
2. Cross out the ones you know are wrong entirely.
3. Think about what remains.
4. Now, write three things you believe about yourself now. They can be different versions of what remains on the first list or something entirely different.
5. On a different piece of paper, write only the three things you believe about yourself now.
6. Cross out anything negative or edit the negative to be a positive. (For example, if you put you are a mean person, change it to "I strive to be kind.")
7. Once you have the positive list, copy it on a clean sheet of paper. Tear up the other sheets and throw them away.
8. Read your remaining list out loud.

9. Post your list somewhere you'll see it every day.

Here's why it works. First, you're updating your core beliefs to reflect who you are now. Second, when you turn the negatives into positives, you're writing positive affirmations you can naturally grow into. Third, by throwing away the old beliefs, you're empowering yourself to move on. And finally, by posting your remaining list somewhere visible, you're reminding yourself in a tangible way how you want to live your life according to your core beliefs, becoming empowered, inspired and motivated to do so.

Remember when I said nurturing your inspiration and motivation takes work? Yeah. This is what I was talking about. But make the effort. You are worth the investment.

> *Beneath the beliefs of yesterday,*
> *I uncovered the truth of today,*
> > *seedlings barely poking through soil,*
> > > *stretching towards the light.*
> > *Dust off their tender leaves.*
> > *Put the planter by the window.*
> > > *Watch them grow.*

Celebrating your core,

Katherine

Falling for the Fake

It's so easy to rely on the external, the transient things that seem to provide inspiration and motivation. Oh, look at the weather. It's so inspiring to walk in the woods! Look at the smile that person gave you. You must be likeable! Don't you feel motivated to do your best now? Look! All these people are following you on social media! They are cheering for you! They love you! Aren't you inspired to keep being the kind, caring, hard-working person you are? Isn't that motivating?

As we've gone through these chapters, we've looked at ways to build motivation and inspiration. We've practiced exercises and thought-provoking activities. Along the way, we said you might experience changes that others can see. What we've been building is internal motivation and inspiration, the kind of thinking that helps you be less reliant on things that change. And that includes people's opinions of you.

Never forget. Even if you are a kind, sincere, hard-working person, just because people like you doesn't mean you will become or remain inspired and motivated. People liking you is external. Your internal thoughts, feelings and actions are what keep you inspired and motivated. And that affects everyone.

Consider this. One morning, the man in the elevator smiles at you. You feel good, right? Boosted and ready to start the day. But the next morning, he ignores you entirely. You don't know what to make of it. You internalize his indifference and wonder. And the next morning, he's frowning. Oh no! That can't be good. You start to worry. What was he thinking? How can you get motivated to make it through a successful day with a start like that?

When you build your inner strength, what is sometimes called intrinsic motivation, you don't have to rely on the weather, your social media followers or the man in the elevator. This doesn't mean you can't derive pleasure from these positive reinforcements or that you can't return affection or that you can't have relationships because people change. It means you begin to see them as nice to have but not always necessary.

Sometimes we believe that if we're kind enough, good enough or authentic enough, everyone will like us. They should, right? I mean, who doesn't like kind, authentic people? Unfortunately, there will always be people who say, "I don't." Maybe they won't say it out loud, but their actions say it for them.

There could be numerous reasons for this, but especially if these folks are acquaintances, it isn't your job to figure out the reason and try to fix it. In fact, trying to fix it because you have a need to be liked is rather selfish. When we do this, we're not doing it for the good of the other person. We're doing it because we rely on their opinion of us. Yikes!

I've learned this the hard way as a business person. Time and time again, I'd get a difficult client. I'd go out of my way for them. I'd even go outside the scope of a contract to keep them happy. Somehow, I believed if I did this, they would like me, and they would appreciate my hard work. The result was always the same. They would continue to take advantage of me, they still wouldn't like me, and I'd end up feeling used and abused.

It's hard to cut ties with someone like that, not just because you keep thinking they will change their minds if you work harder, but because in this case, you need the money, right? It's hard to say money isn't worth it when you are struggling. But here's the thing. If you are struggling, you need to find the inspiration and motivation to get out of that situation. Sometimes, this can be a real challenge.

In my case, I had some options. I worked on pumping myself up to make a leap. I sold my company, got a full-time job and continued to work part-time for the person I sold the company to. Now I was in a position to grow even more because I wasn't reliant on money coming from difficult, unkind people. I was empowered. How did I get there? I had to build up enough confidence to go out and find a job that would work for me. I had to inspire and motivate myself to keep up the search every day. I had to go into an interview and summon every bit of courage I had to show what I had learned and get hired based on my skills, not my ability to be liked.

I still meet unfriendly people. I still meet people who don't like me. It still bothers me. But now, I know my inspiration and motivation do not depend on their attitudes about me if I'm being kind and doing my job. Because I am internally motivated, I am doing the best I've done in my entire life. I'm happier. And that happiness seeps out, positively impacting those around me. That's how powerful internal motivation can be. It's also a testament to how dangerous "fake" external motivation can be.

Here's your homework for this chapter. I'll warn you — it's not easy, and it may leave you with more questions than answers.

1. Make a list of the people who like you, who make you feel so good, you feel like you rely on their good opinion of you.
2. Pick out one person on the list.
3. Visualize how you would feel if they didn't like you for a short period of time.
4. Now, visualize the tools you have in your internal motivation tool chest, and pick some that will help you get past their transient feeling about you.
5. Ask yourself what you would actually do if they didn't like you. Use your internal tools to formulate a creative plan so you don't have to depend on their opinion of you.
6. Look at your plan. Assess whether you could find internal happiness in that plan, at least enough to mentally move on, past their current dislike of you.
7. Think about how that plan makes you feel. It could be a relief. It could be empowering. It could be inspiring or motivating. Or it could be something else.

8. Now, go back and visualize your relationship as it truly stands now. Don't skip this step or you could end up causing yourself unnecessary anxiety.
9. This is crucial: If this exercise gives you anxiety, sadness or lasting feelings of being unsettled, seek guidance from a counselor or therapist right away.

When you build your internal motivation and inspiration to the point at which being liked all the time doesn't determine your happiness, you've gained the kind of confidence you need to move on to a happier life. And that kind of happiness is contagious.

My face formed a smile.
You didn't smile back.
My face formed a frown.
You frowned back.
I turned my back.
Now I smile every day,
either way.
And mostly,
the world smiles, too.

Recognizing the real,

Katherine

Maintenance Work

Few things are more frustrating to me than paying for car repairs. There's always this feeling that I'm paying for the invisible. I want the car to run, I don't really understand what's wrong, but I know I need to pay a lot of money to keep it from breaking down again.

We all have those invisible repairs we need to make, and keeping up with them can be, at the very least, annoying. Maintaining your inspiration and motivation might be one of those things. But if you don't want to break down in the middle of life's highway, it's best to do some maintenance work.

I've talked about using skills like time management, visualization and mindfulness throughout this book. And I've provided exercises to support building those skills in order to keep motivated and inspired to enjoy a happier life. Here's what you do to maintain your success.

1. Go back and circle or bookmark the exercises that you felt gave you the greatest results. It might just be one, and that's OK. If it's more than five, write down all your selections. Then rate them and pick the top five.
2. Each day, practice one of your selected exercises until you feel a) you no longer need that exercise or b) it's no longer giving you the results you need.
3. Repeat steps 1 and 2.
4. This is important: Each time you repeat an exercise, clear your mind of previous results. Approach the exercise as if this is the first time you're doing it. If you don't do this, negative thoughts ("This isn't working.") could prohibit success.

Now, don't be discouraged. You aren't going to be happy all the time. You can't possibly maintain motivation and inspiration every hour of every day. Life's not like that. But you can realistically reach for goals. For me, a comfortable goal is

80/20. If I'm generally happy or even content roughly 80% of the time, I feel I'm doing well. The other 20% is what I'm addressing through these exercises. If that 20% goes up to something like 50% then I sound the alarm. Something is really wrong, and it needs to be addressed directly and immediately. Anything higher than 50 and I know I need some professional support.

I use numbers, but maybe your scale will look differently. Maybe your scale will include colors or emojis or bar graphs. Maybe you'll assess your success by tracking your behaviors and reactions. It doesn't matter. The point is to check in with yourself, see how you're doing and address issues accordingly. That's all part of regular maintenance. It's part of holding on to the progress you've made so you can continue to move forward.

> *On came the "check engine" light.*
> *On came that feeling of "not again."*
> *On came the call to the mechanic*
> *who knows my car and me.*
>
> *Lift the hood.*
>   *Look inside.*
> *Use the tools to twist and turn*
> *those parts that need replacing.*
> *There. It's running again, see?*
>   *Now step on the gas*
>   *and go.*

Yours in lasting inspiration and motivation,

Katherine

Conclusion

When I started this book, I had one objective: to help bring greater happiness to the world by improving on the original book *Get Happy, Dammit*. It was that simple — or so I thought. But when I dug deeper, I realized something. You can do a lot of things to help yourself get happy, but those things have to have relevance and energy. And what has more relevance and energy than that which keeps us inspired and motivated?

While I am a successful writer now, it has been a long road, battling depression, anxiety and PTSD. I've experienced homelessness, living through an abusive relationship, surviving on food stamps and corn muffins and parenting two little ones on my own. That all sounds very sad, but as The Buddha said, "It is to the one who endures that the final victory comes." Thanks to having had a hard-working mother with a perpetually positive attitude, the unexpected blessing of later meeting my amazing spouse and his loving family, and good healthcare and education, I have been able to move beyond it. I remain inspired and motivated. Every day, I work to maintain that.

I regret nothing — indeed, I don't believe in regret. These experiences have brought with them insight I could not have hoped for were they not part of my personal journey. I offer them as examples so you can understand that hope is possible, and even in the worst of times, you can still glean the inspiration and motivation you need to get through life if you incorporate what's meaningful into your thoughts and actions. A small, positive act performed every day can improve mindset and outcomes and make us happier, more fulfilled people.

We create ourselves in layers,
molding those thin, happy moments
between every breath,
each day sticking to our fingers,
forming a second skin.
The glorious waxwork of living.

No matter where you are on your path to achieving your goals, I hope you take care of your mind. It's precious. And I do hope you do what it takes to maintain your motivation and inspiration. They are the ingredients of happiness.

Katherine

About the Author

Katherine Mercurio Gotthardt, M.Ed., writing concentration, hails from the Northern Virginia/D.C. metro area. A writer by nature and by trade, she began writing as soon as her mother helped teach her to read. Katherine's first published poem, "Remembering Thoreau," appeared in *ELF: Eclectic Literary Forum* in in the early 1990s. *Yankee* magazine published "To my Unborn Child" a few years later. Since then, her work has appeared in dozens of magazines, journals, anthologies, books and online media, and her poetry has been taught in secondary and post-secondary classrooms and workshops. To date, she has authored 11 books and has won numerous local, regional and national writing awards.

Well aware of the impact poverty and inequity have on individuals and the community, Katherine uses sales from her books to support local initiatives designed to improve health and wellness for the disadvantaged. All donations are made directly to non-profits or through advocates working within the community.

When she is not writing or volunteering, Katherine spends time enjoying nature and relaxing with her husband, rescue animals and adult children.

Learn more at KatherineGotthardt.com.

Made in the USA
Middletown, DE
12 August 2022